Pressed

BUT NOT CRUSHED

poetry with a purpose by

BRENDA STARR

PRESSED BUT NOT CRUSHED...

© 2021, Brenda Starr.

Print ISBN: 978-1-09838-6-344
eBook iSBN: 978-1-09838-6-351

Always Remember:

YOU MATTER

2 Corinthians 4: 8 We are hard pressed on every side, but not crushed; perplexed, but not in despair.

If you inherited your ancestors (forefathers) wealth, then you also inherited your ancestors (forefathers) debt.

This book is dedicated to my ancestors (my tribe) that survived or did not survive the Middle passage, slavery, racial terror, lynching, Buck breaking, brutalization, discrimination, economic deprivation, poverty, substandard education, segregation, redlining, Jim Crow, and racial injustice that persists in the United States of America to the present day.

CONTENTS

Introduction

I am an American Descendant of Slaves (ADOS), (term founded by Yvette Carnell and Antonio Moore). Foundational Black American (FBA) (term founded by Tariq Nasheed) or as Dr Claude Anderson coined the term "native blacks". I will use the terms African American, blacks, ADOS, FBA, or "native blacks" throughout the book.

I have a clinical diagnosis of non-combatant Post Traumatic Stress Disorder based on trauma that occurred due to a childhood of economic deprivation, abuse, poverty, social depredation, sub-standard education, redlining, discrimination. and systemic racism. The diagnosis of non-combatant PTSD is attributable to the race war black people must fight everyday of our lives.

As I did the research for this book, "Pressed but not Crushed", the history of my/our people is a cause for great sadness to me. The pain of my people, our people, and our history permeated my soul to the point of a deep depression. I had to literally unplug from everything for a period due to ADOS painful history. I had to stop because my soul could no longer stand the pain. I realized that anyone who genuinely CARED and took the time to learn ADOS history would see that we ("native blacks") are in pain and maybe acknowledge that pain. A large majority of Americans do not understand or empathize with "native blacks" pain. Research into the medical community has found the misconception of white physicians who think that "native blacks" do not feel pain. I can assure you not only are we in pain, but we are pained.

I am a baby boomer with one unique caveat. Unlike most baby boomers of my generation, I was raised a Jehovah's' Witness and never went to a church, voted, participated in the civil rights movement, celebrated my birthday, or pledged allegiance to the flag. I was literally raised in a religion that promoted guilt and shame. My mother was an undiagnosed schizophrenic who told me as a child I was smart, but she never told me I was black and the implications of being black in America. My mother was from Mississippi, and I have often wondered why she never told me that unless it was to ensure that I did not carry being black as a stigma in my attempts at becoming a successful person in this society. Society quickly taught me I was black and made sure I understood what that meant. I do not remember the ah ha moment of finding out that I was black but make no mistake, White Supremacy taught me that I was different because I was black, in addition to being raised a Jehovah's Witness.

During the COVID pandemic I emerged as a racial equality activist in the struggle of my/our people. I had like most black people become complacent with United States abuse, brutality, and murder of ADOS living within my social amnesia until the death of George Floyd. I was in a slumber, but that metamorphic incident changed everything.

I am a Christian who believes in God, and he has caused a transformative change as it relates to me and the struggle of my people for racial equality, justice, opportunity and for ADOS economic empowerment. God has inspired me to give birth to this book and has defined my future purpose as it relates to my people. I say I gave birth to this book because I have never felt pain like this since childbirth which was over when my daughter was born. The pain I carry now is chronic and unrelenting and will persist until my people, our people achieve equality, justice, economic empowerment social resources and reparations for our ancestor's labor that built the wealth of this country. This is my prayer:

Prayer for White Supremacy

Most Precious Lord, My God, Heavenly Father. I come to you with thanksgiving and praise-not to be a bother.

God I am humbled by your mercy, and grace-You see our struggle in this country related TO RACE. Lord law enforcement is littered with white supremacists. They are like the federal states who were secessionist-they claim they are Christians', yet they lynch and kill us.

The collaboration of our own people should be discussed. They have taught us to hate ourselves perpetuating our own oppression among us.

Father, white supremacists are so hateful and diabolical-With you on our side ADOS will be unstoppable.

O Lord, my Lord, Oh God most high. I bend my knees and lift my hands to the sky. Praying for ADOS to get to the promised land. Where equality and justice protect the "native black (wo)man".

We have endured horrific violence in addition to taking away our freedom. The tide is about to turn, a new generation, a new season, "The Promised Land", America, Land of the free, excludes ADOS-blatant hypocrisy.

God, we have been patient waiting for over 400 years-Yet we find our condition has not changed what this country owes us is in arrears. God, you have delivered the Jews from Egypt and the Jewish holocaust. ADOS need deliverance from racism in America at any cost.

Lord we put this issue in your hands and authority, Confound the wise by helping us dismantle White Supremacy.

Amen

Acknowledgements

I would first like to thank God for putting the contents of this book into my spirit. I give all glory and honor to God the Father. I thank God for bringing me to where I am today. I discovered a love for gospel music and Mahalia Jackson's," How I Got Over" has become my theme song because I often wonder how I made it this far. Second, I would like to acknowledge Professor Black Truth and The Black Authority. When I started this journey of learning my true history after being in a social amnesia slumber for years, I feel God led me to the New Black Media, a grass roots effort, one of which is the Black Channel which not only aided the learning of my history and current events but helped me understand my history in the context of the racist society in which I currently live. Professor Black Truth and the Black Authority speaks truth about ADOS issues that have been invaluable in helping me gain insights into "native Blacks" circumstances today in our society. The Black Channel film on Race War and Gentrification is a must see (all his productions are excellent). Third, I would like to acknowledge Tariq Nasheed and his stellar film on Buck Breaking. I had an idea for a poem on Buck Breaking but I waited until Tariq published his film to write this poem. Buck Breaking is in the beginning of the book but was one of the last poems I wrote after reviewing the film Buck Breaking. Any ADOS interested in their history, current events, and politics as they relate to ADOS and our efforts to correct the injustice FBA face. I am providing the links to Professor Black Truth/The Black Authority and Tariq Nasheed check out the you tube channels below. This is not an inclusive list of the grassroots New Black Media, however, I was most impressed with the three channels listed below.

- http://theblackchannel.net/
- http://www.youtube.com/user/theblackauthority
- http://www.youtube.com/channel/UX61LFwq1EbuNOl.JwCulA
- http://www.youtube.com/c/TariqRadio

STOLEN

`You took our people, our culture, our freedom...put it on a ship. Transported us to strange shores, imprisoned, beaten, and whipped.

Decades of violence, sexual abuse, selling us as commodities...lynching, hanging with a noose. Oppressed and deprived, freed but not free from a racist society and system that terrifies me.

What can we say? What can we do? We fight for the vote, equal justice, better and equal schools. At one time we were promised 40 acres and a mule... We received Jim Crow and white supremacy rule.

The time has come for African American reparations, for our ancestor's contributions to this nation Our lives were stolen, we were freed but not free. We were branded as" niggers" not fit for white society.

The time has come for African American vindication. Yes America, it is time for black holocaust reparations. Even Germany acknowledged their role in the Jewish holocaust. They recompensed Israel for the millions of Jewish lives lost. Evanston Illinois admits redlining discrimination. They have arranged to pay African American reparations.

America the time has come to acknowledge your racist discrimination. The time has come to provide African American citizens with reconciliation.

We did not ask to be here and now we have been set free, to a life of socioeconomic disadvantage and poverty. Reconciliation and reparation would be a start for the untold numbers of ADOS families torn apart, murdered, and lost.

If indeed we have been totally freed..., Could you take your knee off my neck... because "I can't BREATHE"!

Courtesy the National Memorial for Peace and Justice

Buck Breaking

The antebellum slave masters had some disgusting practices. Buck breaking, (raping "native Black men") a horrendous tactic.

Buck breaking was an exercise in power and dominance. It was meant to break the spirit of the man and take away his confidence.

His humiliation was put on public display. To show the other slaves if they did not behave there would be a terrible price to pay.

The psychological trauma from slavery persists. Native Blacks are raped in prison and branded convicts.

Law enforcements presume all "native blacks" are dangerous and guilty of a crime. It is the sick excuse they use for brutally killing "native blacks" all the time.

Denial is rampant among white supremacists. When you talk about slavery and slavery residuals, they do not want to talk about it.

They want to pretend and tried to teach us slavery was based on biblical principles. They claim they rescued native blacks from being savages, but when we were freed, the narrative changed to "native blacks" are criminals.

We will not let you change or adulterate the actual historical conversation. That shines the light on racism in this so called "land of the free" nation.

National Commission on the Use of Excessive Force

The police reform native blacks were seeking through the establishment of a Presidential commission, has turned into white supremacist bait and switch. Biden promised to confront racial equity, but somehow that plan got ditched.

Of course, Democrats and Republicans cannot agree-whether the legislation will include qualified immunity.

The agenda "native blacks" wanted on police reform-banning chokeholds and qualified immunity continues to be ignored.

White supremacy is just two sides of the same coin. Whether Democrat or Republican, "native blacks" rights are purloined.

If a Commission were formed it would take away White Supremacy Rights, to continue to oppress "native Blacks" and violate their civil rights.

Republican-Democrat-a juxtaposition. Two sides of the same coin, like reciprocal inhibition.

The truth is Biden never planned Executive Police Reform as an administration focus. Forming a Presidential commission on policing is just further white supremacist hocus pocus.

Forming an Executive Commission was just more bait and switch. They continue to use the same white supremacist playbook, ain't that a b!!!!!!

Slave Patrol

What law enforcement needs to understand, that slavery is no longer the law of the land.

The slave patrol is the model on which law enforcement is based. It is designed to single out people of the African American Race.

It is bad enough we were brought here involuntarily, now we must endure the indignities of white supremacy.

The law enforcement system needs a new model, based on dignity and human rights, we should not have to grovel.

The slave patrol with emancipation should be over, Dismantle the current system so our people can have some closure.

From being brutalized, murdered and lynched at the whims of white supremacists. White supremacy has always been, the African Americans nemesis.

Courtesy the Peace and Justice Memorial Center
The National Memorial for Peace and Justice

Courtesy the National Center for Civil and Human Rights
Jim Crow

Slumber

I was in a slumber for over 60 years. When I awakened, I cried emotional tears! The earth is plagued with a COVID 19 pandemic. Systemic Racism in America continues to be an epidemic.

George Floyd awakened me dying, begging for his life. The pain his murder caused our people cut like a knife. Breonna Taylor was an innocent paramedic. She was shot to death in her home and the police were unapologetic.

Lord I want to go back to my slumber. Our plight demands we disencumber from racism and injustice that has been holding us back. The unlimited suffering, we endure, just because we are black.

All these incidents have become a catalyst, for this writer to become a racial equality activist.

Denial

A problem exists for society today. Denial of the issue will not make it go away. Racism permeates every state in the nation. Yet many continue to wonder at African American's frustration.

Opportunities denied, human rights violated, living in public housing, social depredation.

Denial.... Denial they will not admit, that since the 13th amendment was writ-Blacks have been victims of oppression-segregated, lynched, mistreated. Without question.

Yet denial continues to show its ugly face–Denying all the societal issues related to race. If denial could ever be overcome–The war on racism could be won.

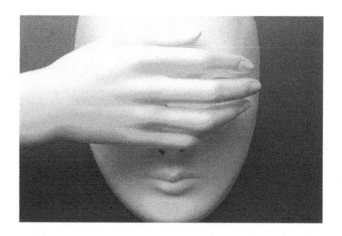

Denial, Denial

Courtesy the National Center for Civil and Human Rights

It is all Lies.

We were told we are sub-human, less than, Niggers. But it is all Lies.

You tried to create a version of what a nigger should be like who is free, and for good measure you lynched what you thought were unrepentant niggers, hanging from a tree.

Your lies continue to this day. You murder us without conscience, seems like a new "native black" person every other day.

No matter how much you hate me, not matter how much you try to segregate me, my very existence is testimony to your lies.

You have degraded our people, treated us worse than animals. The United States was built on the backs of black people. The labor was free and then as chattel property we were deemed valuable.

Once we were set free and our labor started to cost-You told lies we were lazy, stupid, and criminal because you were no longer the boss.

All your lies have persisted to this day-framing misperception of "native blacks" with minstrel and blackface.

Just because you say it does not make it true. It is like your history of America filled with untruths. You wiped away our culture and identity. Then you fought a civil war to keep slaves from being freed.

You stole our inventions and patents, credited them to white people. The injustice imposed on our people is pure evil.

We must confront the lies that you have told. Denial is rampant among you, but you have been exposed.

Stop lying about the oppression you have imposed upon us. It is time to have a discussion.

A discussion that confronts the lies have been told, to keep African Americans "under control".

Remember what is hidden will always be brought to light-As we are exposing the truth as we continue our struggle and fight.

Courtesy the National Center for Civil and Human Rights
Courtesy the National Center for Civil and Human Rights Jim Crow

Immune

We had become immune to "Negroes being put in their place". Until Trayvon, Breonna, and George Floyd were murdered, what a disgrace.

The only thing we have asked for is equality-in education and justice and access to opportunity.

We are at a transformative and defining moment. This country needs to provide atonement.

No longer will we stay or be" put in a negros place". No longer will we allow our people to be debased. The time has come to take a stand, for equality as citizens of this land.

Hate

So much hate in the world, antipathy. So much naked hostility. For anything different from established norms. The fabric of society has been torn.

From the societal tear pours fear and hate. It has accumulated so long it has begun to stagnate.

The solution to hate is unity and love, something this world need a lot more of.

Love will always triumph over hate. Unity and love-lets conversate.

**Courtesy the National Memorial for Peace and Justice-
Soil from the lynching sites occurring in Alabama.**

Pressed
but not Crushed.

The storms of adversity, hurling, whirling crashing through my life, refining me in preparation to fight the good fight.

In the shadow of the Almighty in whose secret place I dwell, the strength of His Majesty speaks "It is well".

The blood of Christ has set me free. God said His grace is sufficient for me. Though I have been through many trials and tribulations, Jesus remains and will always be my vindication.

When I am weak, then I am strong, I mount up with wings like eagles singing "a brand-new song".

As the storms of adversity continue to rage, I recognize the Lord Almighty as my only Sage. Adversity has pressed but not crushed my soul, a new creature in Christ emerges whom God has made whole.

Courtesy the Memorial for Peace and Justice
Lynching Memorials for the State of Illinois

Brown Ebony Girl

Brown Ebony girl you have been shown, your skin is a barrier to your future goals. Your hair is just not good enough. Your Cushite features makes life in America tough.

Life has served you of platter of lies. To sow doubts about your black heritage and pride. Brown Ebony girl you should know-the cradle of civilization is your celebrity cameo.

Brown Ebony girl your beauty really has no rival. In fact, you need to understand that for your survival. In a country that caters to race, a country where we are oppressed and brutalized to be kept in our place.

Know that you are beautiful and strong. You must stand up to right the wrongs; imposed on our people when they were stolen-bought to this land whipped, beaten, and broken.

Robbed of culture, dignity, and identity. Treated in this country as a non-entity.

Brown Ebony girl hold up your chin, even when people act like you do not fit in. The world cannot stop you from shinning your light. So other Brown Ebony skin people can see and join the fight.

The fight to dissolve this construct called race, an unending battle that Brown Ebony skin people face.

Guardians of Racism

Guardians of Racism, also known as the Supreme Court-Its rulings and decisions has made killing "native blacks" a sport.

You upheld Jim Crow laws in the Southern states-Plessey vs Ferguson is an example, separate but equal for the races.

The Dredd- Scott landmark decision, denied ADOS the right to be citizens. The Civil Rights Act of 1965, finally helped promote the 14th amendment.

The Supreme Court eviscerated the Voting Act of 1965. Shelby County vs Holder allows Confederate states to suppress ADOS voter rights.

The Supreme Court is supposed to ensure equal justice under the law, however when we appear as plaintiffs on an issue we are treated as outlaws.

But God I believe with you anything is possible. The miracles you have performed could fill a chronicle.

The Judicial Branch of government is stacked with people who see, ADOS as chattel property, they are truly evil.

The Supreme Court Judges enjoy a lifetime appointment. The laws they decide empty rhetoric, to ADOS poignant.

As the Guardians of Racism currently stand, there will never be equal justice for ADOS under the laws of this land.

Mass Incarceration

Slavery was abolished except for a technicality-The thirteenth amendment allows involuntary servitude if duly convicted legally.

The Biden Anti-Drug Abuse law of 1986-created sentencing disparities for" native blacks" that have been unabated since.

The 1994 Violent Crime Control and Law Enforcement Act-The Biden law that promoted building of prisons and incarceration of more native blacks.

Federal incentives for states to enact truth in sentencing laws. Imprisoning Foundational Black Americans interminably, the whole process is a fraud.

Foundational Black Americans are criminally guilty until proven innocent-The Courts are accomplices in "native Black" Americans false imprisonment.

Convict leasing is a term no longer used today-UNICOR, Federal Prison Industry programs legally subjugates inmates in this age.

The 13th amendment justifies slavery for criminal punishment. Labor laws do not apply equally, enforced labor, unequal justice.

Mass incarceration is white supremacist engineered it is time to be reversed. Incentivize crime and mass incarceration reduction, get rid of three strikes. Give the mass incarcerated population a chance at a free and new life.

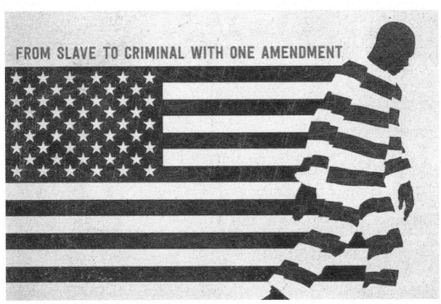

FROM SLAVE TO CRIMINAL WITH ONE AMENDMENT

This Photo by Unknown Author is licensed under CC BY-NC-ND

Qualified Immunity

Carte blanche permission to use deadly force. Law enforcement uses this Supreme Court ruling to kill Blacks without remorse.

The Supreme Court continues to uphold this over 50-year-old legal doctrine. An Ill-conceived-doctrine, misbegotten.

For once Clarence Thomas dissented in African Americans favor. He condemned the Supreme Court for their racist behavior.

I am so tired of the violence against my people and me. "Say their names" could fill a book you see.

Systematic racism-racial injustice, murdering" native black" children, women, and men has become a constant in this country.

Black people cherish equality and justice however, brutality and violence still engulf us.

Qualified immunity, another tool of white supremacy, for ADOS born and oppressed in the land of the "so called" free.

This is not who we are?

Tamir Rice, dead, age twelve, murdered by law enforcement, those were the cards he was dealt.

Sandra Bland, questions still arise, about her murder the coroner ruled was a suicide.

White Kyle Rittenhouse shot and killed two people and walked away. Jacob Blake was shot in the back seven times that same day.

This is not who we are you say. Wake up America, systemic racism has always been the mainstay.

The Dred Scott decision denied African Americans citizenry. This is who you are America, this is your history.

African American brutalization, violation of human rights. Characterized as sub-humans not equal to whites.

Perpetuating the lie that there is equality and justice for all, NOT TRUE, we decry, admit the shortfall.

This is who you are look, admit it. Once accountability is established you will no longer be a hypocrite.

All we ask is to be treated with human dignity, equality and justice, a privilege we have been denied since we were abducted.

The Confederate Flag

When you wave the Confederate flag, it says to me, you view African Americans as a piece of property.

Property you can own and treat anyway you like. This has always been the African Americans plight.

You say the flag is a part of your heritage and history. We say it represents how you terrorized us and tried to block efforts to set African Americans free.

Let us settle the issue once and for all. The Confederate flag represents a society in which we are considered unequal.

Your insouciant attitude about how African Americans have been treated, has been the norm since we have received our freedom.

To us the Confederate flag is a symbol of hate, it says you are attempting to recreate,

A system in which we do not have any rights. A system that promotes the superiority of whites.

Problematic Images

Retiring Uncle Ben, Retiring Aunt Jemima, Change the names of baseball teams to acknowledge,

Systematic racism, problematic images, America's racism has no limits. It is going to take more than changing names or faces. American oppressors need to offer African American reparations and reconciliation.

African Americans were robbed of culture, dignity, and identity. Then you tried to rewrite our history.

Your history reveals America the strong white nation, your history minimizes slavery and corralling Indians onto reservations.

Removing "problematic images" will not solve the problem. Reforming systematic racism, now that would be a fruitful outcome.

Once America can let go of their social amnesia and face up to the real reason,

There is so much inequality among Blacks because of your structural hegemony.

H.R. 40

A bill that wants to appoint a commission to investigate this country Americas omission-to right the wrong of slavery imposed on my ancestors, by the United States colonial oppressors.

Can't you just do the research and see-the damage slavery has caused this society. The development of the construct called race-developed to keep African Americans in their place.

Years of unspeakable hate, cruelty, and inequality-It influences ADOS people who were legally set free". HR 40 is designed to explore the question, of an apology from America and measures to right the transgression.

Personally, I think this bill is an insult. It was written in 1989 pulled out periodically and dangled like a carrot in front of a horse.

We do not need a study and if we did an Executive order would suffice. White supremacy has no intention of easing "native blacks" strife.

So, let us not continue to pretend Congress will pass a bill written in 1989. Which does not have ADOS interests in mind.

We see through the sham, we see through the collaborators, that insist on pushing a nonsensical bill while collaborating with White supremacists who hates us. H.R. 40 a classic smoke and mirror. It does not address our issues or White supremacy's reign of terror.

If you genuinely want us to have reparations, get rid of HR 40 and give us true legislation. Legislation that addresses ADOS history. Legislation that should have been passed when ADOS were set free.

When I first wrote this poem, it was to be an educational tool describing H.R. 40. I am not a proponent of H.R. 40 as our people are way past a commission. An executive order could set up this commission if it were truly desired by the legislature and President Biden. I feel we need to go directly to the remedy of economic empowerment, social resources, equal opportunity and equal justice needed to address American Descendants of Slaves. A bill that has been around since 1989 is defunct and if information is required about our history and what the residuals of slavery are, just ask Bryan Stevenson who has done all the research through the Equal Justice Initiative, the Legacy Museum and the National Memorial for Peace and Justice.

I

116TH CONGRESS
1ST SESSION

H. R. 40

To address the fundamental injustice, cruelty, brutality, and inhumanity of slavery in the United States and the 13 American colonies between 1619 and 1865 and to establish a commission to study and consider a national apology and proposal for reparations for the institution of slavery, its subsequent de jure and de facto racial and economic discrimination against African-Americans, and the impact of these forces on living African-Americans, to make recommendations to the Congress on appropriate remedies, and for other purposes.

IN THE HOUSE OF REPRESENTATIVES

JANUARY 3, 2019

Ms. JACKSON LEE (for herself, Mr. SERRANO, Mr. COHEN, Mr. KHANNA, Mr. MEEKS, Ms. MOORE, Ms. JAYAPAL, Mr. JOHNSON of Georgia, Mr. PAYNE, Ms. CLARKE of New York, Ms. JOHNSON of Texas, Mrs. BEATTY, Ms. SCHAKOWSKY, Mr. THOMPSON of Mississippi, Ms. LEE of California, Mr. GREEN of Texas, Ms. NORTON, Mr. RUSH, Mr. NADLER, Mr. DANNY K. DAVIS of Illinois, Mr. ENGEL, Mr. RICHMOND, Ms. BASS, and Mr. EVANS) introduced the following bill; which was referred to the Committee on the Judiciary

---

A BILL

To address the fundamental injustice, cruelty, brutality, and inhumanity of slavery in the United States and the 13 American colonies between 1619 and 1865 and to establish a commission to study and consider a national apology and proposal for reparations for the institution of slavery, its subsequent de jure and de facto racial and economic discrimination against African-Americans, and the impact of these forces on living African-Americans,

COVID-19

The world is infected, we are amidst a pandemic,

The origin Wuhan, China, a COVID-19 epidemic.

To control the outbreak requires simple public health measures. It requires us as American citizens to all come together.

Naysayers will not wear masks and claim their personal freedom-the constitution being the primary reason.

It seems not to matter that other people are affected, by disregard of public health principle leaving the vulnerable unprotected.

Americans are lining up to receive free food. The government is guilty of moral turpitude.

Impending loss of a place to live, unemployment is rampant, something must give.

Vaccines have been approved and I am sorry to say, that disenfranchised people have not been given the vaccine right away.

As usual the disenfranchised are the last to receive, the lifesaving COVID-19 vaccine.

Executive Orders and Memos 2021

A new term has been coined, the term is racial equity and justice, an executive order was written for racial equity that does not mention us.

Before the election African American Women were the backbone of the Democratic party. Now the elections over those women are at the bottom of the hierarchy,

We have endured white supremacy for over four hundred years. America's debt owed to African Americans is financially in arrears.

Advancing equity for all African Americans are not specifically mentioned. Reparations? Not being given any attention.

Asian's, Pacific Islanders, and immigrants are prominent in the executive order. The Democratic Party some African Americans supported, did not support us.

Of all the African American people that have been lynched and murdered. Asians and Pacific Islanders took number one in the rank order.

Suddenly everything is for people of color and the underserved-We know bait and switch when we see it, we are and have always been the true "underserved".

We have seen this cycle before, wash, rinse, repeat. African Americans always have taken the back seat.

Biden said the disproportionate number of COVID cases among African Americans are not white people's fault. If that is true what is systemic structural racism all about?

An order to protect Asian's and Pacific Islanders as citizens. An order that specifically omits African Americans, that is significant.

As always, we are last on the list. We will continue to fight; we will continue to persist.

We do not need a study consistent with applicable laws to assess, why this country has never taken its knee off ADOS neck.

Capitol Riot

Trump supporters started at riot at the capital. It was well planned sedition; the tension was palpable.

Law enforcement socialized with the rioters, and they built gallows with a noose, a reminder to African Americans that lynching could be reintroduced.

Law enforcement kindly escorted rioters out of the people's house. They did not even arrest them or take them to the jailhouse.

The double standard of justice in this country continues to be revealed. America you can no longer conceal, how they treat African Americans is inconsistent, with how they treat white domestic terrorists, it is a contradiction.

We learned that police do not have to kill" native blacks". The rioters were treated with great respect.

Which begs the question how come we are always being murdered, when White Supremacist storming the capitol and living to talk about it is a threat of no small order.

The Senate has impeached the 45th President, The Republicans however continue to dissent. The standard for justice is different you see, for representatives of white supremacy.

Unprecedented!!!!

The word most associated with the Trump Administration-
Unprecedented!

The largest audience to ever witness an inauguration, period?
Unprecedented!

Campaign style speech using the CIA Memorial Wall as a prop
Unprecedented!

A Muslim ban signed in the Pentagon Hall of Heroes.
Unprecedented!

Secretary Tillerson fired on social media.
Unprecedented!

Decision making based on gut feelings.
Unprecedented!

Reality is negotiable.
Unprecedented!

The longest government shutdown in history.
Unprecedented!

Children separated from their family and incarcerated in cages.
Unprecedented!

The press is the enemy of the people.
Unprecedented!

Jamal Khashoggis' murder ignored.
Unprecedented!

Nepotism in the White House.
Unprecedented!

Dishonoring Americans Veterans.
Unprecedented!

Unlimited propaganda, hoaxes, and fake news.
Unprecedented!

There were good people on both sides in Charlottesville.
Unprecedented!

A President who does not release tax returns.
Unprecedented!

Fired from office by African Americans.
Unprecedented!

New lexicon "shithole countries".
Unprecedented!

Only President to be impeached twice.
Unprecedented!

Republicans do not want to hold him responsible for the Capitol riots.
Unprecedented!

This President has been a blight on the nation, with the Make America Great Again (white supremacist) fixation.

Say Their Names...

SAY THEIR NAMES LIST 2021 📢 #SayTheirNames (sayevery.name)

**I have found when I am trying to be inclusive,
some people find that intrusive.**

Kalief Browder

Kalief Browder

Imprisoned for 3 Years Without A Conviction

HUFF POST LIVE

Stopped and frisked by law enforcement for allegedly stealing a backpack. Kalief Browder was never able to get his life back.

The law says you are innocent until proven guilty. Kalief was sixteen years old and charged as an adult with grand larceny.

He was held in solitary confinement for over two years, suffering indignity and humiliation, yet somehow, he persevered.

For three years they encouraged him to take a deal, for a backpack Kalief insisted he did not steal.

Kalief would not let them make him into a criminal. The horror of his treatment at Rikers Island was despicable.

The prosecution could never produce a witness. They never really had any evidence to convict him.

He was at Rikers Island for three years and his case was dismissed. The terror from his incarceration experience continued to persist.

His depression from being brutalized caused him to take his own life. He was only 22 years old when he took flight.

The Capitol riot exposed everything we have been trying to say, about unequal justice and treatment "native blacks" face every day.

They have released Capitol rioters like Stephanie Hazelton on unsecured bonds. Some sent home with ankle monitors to prevent attempts to abscond.

One rioter was given bail and given judicial permission to go to Mexico-Is this reminiscent of the Old "Jim Crow"?

Kalief's story and his time in jail-Demonstrates why we need sweeping reforms that would end cash bail.

End Cash Bail

Sandra Bland

Stopped for changing lanes without a signal, Sandra Bland was taken to jail.

Three days later they allegedly they found her hanging in her cell.

Sandra Bland was outspoken about her rights. She did not know that it would cost her, her life.

Her fingerprints or DNA were not even on the plastic garbage bag noose. The evidence and crime scene they manufactured was a ruse.

The autopsy showed that she was hung. We are still being lynched in 2021.

The alternate facts Waller County presented, claimed she hung herself because she was tormented.

You tried to create a narrative for Sandra that did not exist, our people know better, and we will persist.

To expose what happened to a young African America woman. Lynched in Texas for being outspoken.

Breonna Taylor

A beautiful young woman, not even in her prime. Sleeping at home while black should not be a crime.

Yet law enforcement rammed their way into her house, with a no knock warrant they later lied about.

Thirty-two shots were fired by law enforcement, six went into Breonna. Her young body could not withstand that trauma. As she lay dead on the floor, her heart to beat nevermore.

They did not even search the house. So, what was the warrant all about. The report they wrote did not even mention, the homicide the coroner determined was committed.

The law enforcement committing the homicide were not arrested, and yet some people questioned why we protested.

One of our supposed kin, who really cares nothing for our melanin skin, convened a grand jury and never said her name. America and Kentucky, have you no shame?

We are continuing to fight for a fair outcome, that favors justice for our loved ones.

If a person cannot be safe in their own house, then what is civil rights all about?

Ahmad Arbery

Lynching has not been outlawed in this country. Modern lynching is happening against African American men and women, I am telling you this fact bluntly.

Ahmad Arbery was out for a run, cornered by a car and truck and three white men with guns.

They murdered Ahmd Arbery and tried to say, they were doing a citizen's arrest and he was trying to get away.

The murderers lied and said there had been robberies in the neighborhood and they were looking out for the "greater good".

They did not arrest the men and took them at their word, until the video surfaced, and Ahmad could be seen and heard.

Jim Crow is supposed to be over. We as an emancipated people need closure.

To the historic racial disparities and social injustice, imposed on us by law enforcement.

Lynching needs to be outlawed in any form, equal justice and rights for African Americans should be the norm.

We cannot keep having what happened to Emmet Till. Congress needs to pass legislation, to protect "native blacks" the Emmet Till anti-lynching bill.

George Floyd

It is a medical fact the brain cannot live without oxygen. Four minutes is the usual constant.

The brain dies without oxygen within 4-6 minutes. Nine minutes and twenty-nine seconds is way beyond the limit.

Georges trip to Cup foods would be the last in his life. Video evidence reveals to the world ADOS strife.

As he pleaded "I can't breathe", Derek Chauvin continued to press his knee. George Floyd has become a catalyst for lifting the social amnesia; affecting us as black people, we need a panacea.

What happened to George Floyd was just not right, but in his honor, we continue to fight.

We will fight for the right to live in our skin, without being murdered again, and again.

Finally White supremacists sacrificed one of their own, because "native blacks" have stepped up and shown we have a backbone.

Derek Chauvin was found guilty, a triumph for us, but with all the murders happening it is still not enough. The United States should not try to chastise anyone about human rights, until they deal with the inhumane treatment "native blacks" receive from supremacist whites.

Trayvon Martin

Rest in Power Trayvon

Travon means "Gift of God, Illuminating" like the sun. That is who Trayvon Martin was. George Zimmerman extinguished his light after chasing him down and starting a fight.

His journey on earth was cut short, He took a stand as a last resort.

George Zimmerman is autographing skittles, the trial for Trayvon's murder. he received a judicial acquittal.

His death is a rallying call to our community, to STAND OUR GROUND with impunity.

Black Lives Matter, there is so much injustice. Black Lives Matter a new movement a new compass.

We are Trayvon, shot in the heart, we are Trayvon his living counterpart.

We will not let this country forget, why African ADOS feel a constant threat of death.

We are Trayvon, we have his complexion. We are sick and tired of ADOS oppression.

Black Live Matters now our mantra. We will say and display it like the national anthem.

REST IN POWER!

Tamir Rice

Rest in Power Tamir. We will not forget!

Tamir Rice was an African American twelve-year-old boy. Shot dead by law enforcement for playing with a toy.

It still saddens our people deeply to this day, law enforcement who murdered him were told it was OK.

Law enforcement justified this murder, saying he was a black male who was lethal, but the video proved they were being deceitful.

Tamir did not realize in this so called "land of the free", that an African American twelve-year-old could be treated so atrociously.

We can no longer endure this pain in silence. The humiliation, pain, and suffering our people experience because of law enforcement violence.

Bryan Steven's National Memorial for Peace and Justice should establish a new category, of modern lynching methods employed, someone needs to memorialize this story.

The criminal murder of a twelve-year-old boy, who was doing what children do, playing with a toy.

Jamar Mackey

He was sitting "while black" at the mall eating a meal with his family. Up walks the police and slap handcuffs on him denying him a right to be free. He asks why-they tell him he fits the description, of a black man reported in the mall grifting.

This is a mistake-He tries to explain, they do not listen, they continue to arrest and try to take him to prison. How much longer do we have the endure the indignity perpetuated by law enforcement which treats African Americans differently?

When all was said and done- it turned out he was not the one. His family was terrorized all for nothing, the dehumanizing behavior and racist attitudes are so insulting.

There needs to be some actual enforceable reform to correct the systemic racism of those wearing police uniforms. I am not safe on the street, at home, or at the mall. 2020 has become a black killing spree free for all.

But like he said, you will hear from us again. This racial profiling of African American's must end.

Karen

Emmet Till would still be alive today, if a Karen had not told a lie causing his life to be taken away.

Amy Cooper, dubbed a Karen, tried to use the racist system, to turn Christian Cooper into another African American victim.

New York has passed a Klu Klux Karen law, to punish Karen's guilty of basically being outlaws.

Keyon Harold was falsely accused, and assaulted-the antics of Karen's are extremely exhausting.

What is it about our melanin skin, that provokes such hostility and hate to our chagrin?

Technology has now exposed all the lies. African American people cannot continue to be penalized.

For false accusations from racist Karen's, your behavior toward African Americans has become transparent.

We have learned that White women are the worst terrorists. They will get us killed in a minute because they are treacherous.

Do not be fooled by these white women. Who feel this is their country and will have you killed without contrition?

White supremacist women are a dangerous matter. Please do not forget this or you can end up as a cadaver. Karen's, we just want you to know, that we see you for what you are you are, a throwback to Jim Crow.

KÅREN

WE SEE YOU

Black Lives Matter

The Bible says, "what is hidden will be bought to light". Racism permeates our society like a blight.

Denial has always been the response. Black Lives Matter is a new renaissance.

America, America, land of the free, except for people that look like me. Trayvon Martin and COVID-19 is responsible for a new conversation. We really need God to heal this nation.

Confronting the issue is a promising start if we all come together and do our part. As our struggle continues a new movement has been born. Black Lives Matter, we will shout it through a bullhorn.

Song of my Spirit

Holy Spirit.... God in me

Holy Spirit.... a gift to me

Holy Spirit.... sets me free,

And protects me from my enemies.

Holy Spirit...God in me

Holy spirit ...lets me see.

Holy Spirit...groans for me

And breaks the bondage sin has on me.

Holy Spirit... comforts me.

Holy Spirit ...teaches me.

Holy Spirit... Manifest Christ's love in me

The Gift

The greatest gift I have ever received... A tiny seed planted when I conceived. I understand the principle-you sow and then you reap. Nay Sayers advocated abortion, but Mama said this child you will keep.

This child is God's way of giving you a blessing. An enhancement to this life of Christ you are confessing. Despite haters plans to take her away, she was born healthy and beautiful on her birthday. I harvested a crop of bounteous fruit, joy, grace, love, kindness, beauty, sown with deep roots,

A blessing from God, I am humbled and believe, she is truly the greatest gift I have ever received.

Damaged

I was born in poverty without defect-poor, living in public housing, socioeconomically disadvantaged, what a wreck.

Mama was sick in the head. Mama was sick in the bed. Moaning Lord, Lord, have mercy on my soul. Jehovah's witnesses took advantage, promised to make her whole.

I baptize you in the name of the Watchtower Bible and tract society. The brothers on immersion in baptismal water invoke with piety.

Weekly field service, ministry school and other meetings. If our behavior got restless, Mama meted out the beatings.

Guilt and shame became our mantra. We could not pledge allegiance to the flag or sing the national anthem. No Christmas, no birthdays, no Halloween. There were ABSOLUTELY no celebrations and no in between.

Wounded, broken, injured, damaged, How could we as children manage. Life as we knew it was like growing up in a cult. We could not wait to become adults.

All the indignities Jehovah's witnesses poured into us, became useless defense mechanisms as the result.

My siblings and I must work to heal our damage. That will be our ultimate challenge. Their indoctrination was firmly planted in our minds, by a religion where the blind leads the blind.

Testimony

God has given me a testimony-that is singularly mines only.

The trials and tribulations I have had had to bear, assured me that God was always there.

Nothing I have been through has gone to waste, that is due to God's unending grace.

God has used my testimony to help many-I am a soldier in God's army of love to help fight the enemy.

Remember your testimony can be... the one thing that sets a person free,

To experience the love and mercy of Christ-in whom we have been promised an abundant life.

Praying

When I pray I expect things to happen. I sing songs of praise my feet just a tappin.

God is faithful he gives me a garment.... of praise and worship, God's love is so ardent.

Prayers are our form of communication; it is a like fire in my bones burning like capsaicin.

I do not always get the answer I desire-One thing I have found is that God is not a liar.

His promises are firm like the earth on which we stand. I am graced and blessed to be touched by God's hand.

Masks of Abuse

Abuse can wear many masks. Disguised as a child doing the enemies tasks.

I was abused by a hateful manipulative child-her rude and destructive behavior knew no bounds.

She would walk into a room where I was just as cool as you please-scream bloody murder for no reason and mama came with a beating.

When her situation with her mother fell apart-I was there to make sure she had a good start. She readily admits to her abuse. She does not make any excuse.

She has never given me an explanation. She has never offered any placation. What is hidden is now bought to light-Abuse done to me because of spite?

The Enemy Within

Such a sin-such a sin. I must overcome the enemy within.

The enemy within my point of origin. The family I must fight a war in. A war to be safe from harm and protected. A war where I am safe not abandoned or rejected.

I already must struggle with a racist and unequal society. I also struggle with the enemy within... my family.

Incest, sexual abuse, physical abuse was rampant. Social checks and balances were mysteriously absent. So much to overcome, it is a shame really, when the enemy within is your own family.

Addiction

Addiction is easy it helps to forget, everything in life for which you have regrets.

It matters not what substance you choose to abuse if the high blots out the issues and the blues.

The only problem when the high goes away, the problems you were running from are still here to stay.

I have found addiction is not the solution. That became apparent during my personal evolution.

Addiction will always offer a place to hide. For those who will not deal with their feelings inside.

My Joy

Creamy Gold-Borne in pain, My Joy comes to me-full of life, laughter, and love.

I look and wonder could it possibly be that this beautiful child is a product of me?

I gather her close, I hold her tight, I kiss her lips, I pinch her thigh. She smiles and then returns my affection; Again, I marvel at such perfection-

In a child, born of me-Who will always without effort be, My Joy.

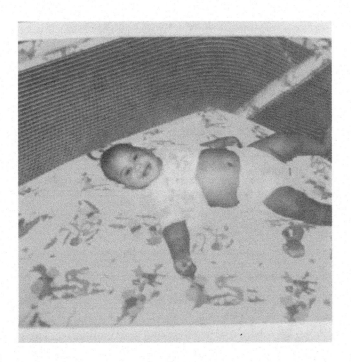

Bryan Stevenson

I learned about a man name Bryan Stevenson, who reminds me of the Apostle Paul. A servant of the Lord who fights for equal justice for all.

Our people are his family, and he cares for us like a father. The work he does for mass incarceration victims for him seems to be an honor. He educates "native blacks" about their legacy. He calls out white supremacy and exposes their heresy.

He established the Legacy Museum and The Memorial for Peace and Justice. These institutions tell the story of our people and how we were abducted.

He uses his skills and knowledge as a lawyer to correct- injustice within the judicial system that is supposed to protect.

Americas has a double standard of law and order. His legacy to our people is a Memorial of our history and how we were murdered.

He has exposed "native blacks" misery to all the injustices in this so-called land of the free, America, the United States, our country.

Although change in this country for ADOS has been slow, he is not deterred he presses forward like a John Deere backhoe.

I could not write this book without an honorable mention-What he has accomplished in his short life defies most people's comprehension.